WHAT EVERY STUDENT SHOULD KNOW ABOUT READING AND STUDYING THE SOCIAL SCIENCES

Sally A. Lipsky
Arden B. Hamer
Indiana University of Pennsylvania

Allyn & Bacon

Boston   Columbus   Indianapolis   New York   San Francisco   Upper Saddle River
Amsterdam   Cape Town   Dubai   London   Madrid   Milan   Munich   Paris   Montreal   Toronto
Delhi   Mexico City   Sao Paolo   Sydney   Hong Kong   Seoul   Singapore   Taipei   Tokyo

Editor-in-Chief: Karon Bowers
Editorial Assistant: Susan Brilling
Marketing Manager: Blair Tuckman
Production Editor: Claudine Bellanton
Editorial Production Service: Pre-Press PMG
Manufacturing Buyer: JoAnne Sweeney
Electronic Composition: Pre-Press PMG
Cover Administrator/Designer: Kristina Mose-Libon

Library of Congress Cataloging-in-Publication Data
Lipsky, Sally.
   What every student should know about reading and studying the
social sciences / Sally A. Lipsky, Arden B. Hamer. — 1st ed.
      p. cm.
   Includes bibliographical references.
   ISBN-13: 978-0-13-714137-1
   ISBN-10: 0-13-714137-8
   1. Social sciences—Study and teaching. 2. Study skills. I. Hamer, Arden B. II. Title.
   H62.L489 2009
   300.71'1—dc22
                                                                 2009017334
10 9 8 7 6 5 4 3 2 1   13 12 11 10 09

**Allyn & Bacon
is an imprint of**

ISBN-10: 0-13-714137-8

www.pearsonhighered.com   ISBN-13: 978-0-13-714137-1

Contents

PREFACE

Many students begin college with little or no guidance about the requirements and expectations of courses in higher education. The purpose of this book is to provide practical information about how to approach and learn content for a college-level Social Science course. This book is best used from the start of the semester as a complement to the text and other course materials. Included in this book are recommended practices for beginning the term, reading and studying from a textbook, listening and taking notes in class, and preparing for exams. Students are expected to apply and evaluate select strategies as they proceed through the semester.

Text Features

- **The Study Cycle,** described in Chapter 1, provides students with a strategic plan for how to approach out-of-class work. With simple yet important steps, the Study Cycle provides a framework by which students utilize the strategies described in subsequent chapters.
- **Select, Sort, and Solidify,** also introduced in Chapter 1, are the three steps integrated throughout subsequent chapters. Learning is a process; these steps provide students with a basis for acquiring a deeper understanding of content in their Social Science course. Specific strategies for selecting, sorting, and solidifying information are presented for chapter topics—textbook reading, in-class note taking, and preparing for exams.
- **Examples** of how students apply the **Select, Sort, and Solidify** process are presented in each chapter. These examples include textbook pages, in-class notes, and study guides and review sheets for a variety of Social Science courses.
- **Student Comments** are interspersed within chapters. The comments are from college students who completed a course in which they had to implement and assess a variety of learning strategies in Social Science courses. Their remarks and suggestions help to guide and motivate beginning college students.

- **Summary Charts,** located at the ends of selected chapters, provide an overview of strategies presented within the chapter. Students are directed to use the chart as they plan approaches for reading and studying content in their Social Science course.
- **Taking Action** is a five-step process that follows each Summary Chart. Students are directed to reflect on and assess information presented in the chapter by applying strategies to a specific assignment, class session, or test. Students check off strategies on a sheet, cut out the sheet, and then use it as a bookmark to remind them of their plan.
- **The Checklist of Strategies,** presented in the last chapter, is a means for students to periodically assess strategies that they have and/or have not implemented in their Social Science course. As a culminating exercise, students **Prioritize and Apply** five strategies that will help them improve the effectiveness and efficiency of their learning.

INTRODUCTION: TO THE STUDENT

The intent of this handbook is to help you make sense of information that you will encounter in your Social Science course, both in the textbook and in the classroom. By following the strategies presented in this book, you will maximize the effectiveness and the efficiency by which you read, study, and learn content for your Social Science course.

What Are the Social Sciences?

The Social Sciences represent branches of learning that study elements of human experience from differing perspectives. The Social Sciences can include a variety of disciplines: Anthropology, Criminology, Economics, Geography, History, Political Science, Psychology, Religious Studies, and Sociology. Professionals in each of these fields have differing viewpoints and approaches toward studying topics. For example, Social Science professionals might examine the topic of **GENDER** accordingly:

- *Anthropologists*—Differences between males and females in western versus non-western cultures.
- *Criminologists*—Profiles and patterns of males and females within a criminal justice system.
- *Economists*—Current spending trends of males and females.
- *Historians*—Impact of females in the work force during and after WWII.
- *Political Scientists*—Civic engagement and voting patterns of males and females.
- *Psychologists*—Behavioral and emotional differences of males and females.
- *Sociologists*—Roles of males and females within and across ethnic groups in our society.

Among the Social Science disciplines there are many overlapping aspects of study. However, you should be mindful of the specialized point of view for the course that you are enrolled in currently. An awareness of the perspective within a Social Science discipline will help you to better understand the content that you are learning. Therefore, as you read the textbook, listen in class, take notes, and prepare for exams in your Social Science course, be aware of the specialized point of view for that subject area.

1

JUMP START THE SEMESTER

The start of a semester can be a confusing and overwhelming time for college students, especially for first-time students. One way to ease initial apprehensions is to approach your college academics as you would a new full-time job. That is, from the start, work at being conscientious, diligent, and productive—you will impress not only your college instructors, but also yourself!

The First Week

- **Attend class.** During the first week of classes, instructors talk about important information not covered again in the semester, such as setup and requirements for the course and explanations about information on the syllabus. Also, many instructors begin lecturing the first day.
- **Read the syllabus.** The syllabus, or course outline, is an important document for all courses. A syllabus is similar to a contract created by the instructor for students. Instructors usually hand out the syllabus during the first class session, or at least the first week of classes. Review the syllabus closely since it provides information about:
  - *Contacting your instructor.* Take note of your instructor's office hours, location of the office, phone number and email address. Also, how does your instructor want you to contact him? Some instructors prefer email; others prefer that you come to their office.

- ◆ *Attendance policy.* Note your instructor's policies regarding class absences. Is class attendance part of your overall grade in the course? What constitutes an "excused" versus an "unexcused" absence? How many classes can you miss before you are penalized? Also, what should you do if you are sick or have a personal emergency—how do you contact your instructor, and how do you get information about missed class work?
- ◆ *Assignments.* Make note of due dates, explanations, and other expectations of the instructor.
- ◆ *Grading.* How will you be evaluated in the course? Be aware of requirements and point values for assignments, papers, projects, quizzes, exams, and any other means of evaluation.
- ◆ *Late assignment policy.* As with class attendance, instructors can have widely differing procedures for turning in late assignments. First, will your instructor accept a late assignment? Will you be penalized for turning in an assignment past the due date? What constitutes a reasonable excuse?

- **Buy textbooks and supplies.** Go to the campus bookstore; this is the most expedient way to purchase texts, supplemental materials (handbooks, DVDs), and supplies. Go early—you will avoid crowds and have a better chance of purchasing used and, therefore, cheaper texts. (Be sure to purchase a copy with the least amount of text marking and highlighting.) Also, keep your sales receipt and do not write in the text until you are sure you will use it for the course. Most bookstores have return policies, including a limited time period by which to return textbooks.
- **Obtain a planner or calendar.** Keep track of academic requirements (assignments, projects, papers, quizzes, exams, class cancellations, extra labs, study/review sessions), as well as personal and social activities. In upcoming weeks, you easily can forget or feel overwhelmed with mounting activities and obligations. Using a planner or calendar daily will help you manage your time and feel a greater sense of control regarding academic and personal responsibilities.
- **Preview the textbook.** Take note of the following features:
  - ◆ *Abbreviated or brief table of contents.* Provides an overview of topics covered in the text.

- *Expanded table of contents.* Provides more details regarding topics and layout of the textbook.
- *Preface or introduction.* The author explains the approach of the text, the main features within the text, and suggested approaches for reading the text.
- *Glossary.* Defines terminology used in the text.
- *Index.* An alphabetical directory of subjects, people, and/or events in the text.
- *Appendix.* Can include answer keys; extra charts, timelines, or other illustrative materials; a list of sources; and other materials to enhance text content.
- *Supplemental materials.* Is there a Website, CD, podcast, or manual that accompanies the text?

Begin the Study Cycle

For the vast majority of students, academic success in college involves considerable more time and effort than in high school. Generally speaking, for *each hour spent in class*, college students should expect to spend 2 hours doing out-of-class work for that course. Thus, for a course that meets 3 hours per week, be prepared to spend 6 hours doing course work out of class. Like many college students, you might be unaware of what specifically you should be doing during this time for out-of-class course work. The **Study Cycle** (below), along with specific strategies described in subsequent chapters, provides you with a strategic plan for your out-of-class work.

The Study Cycle

review lecture notes ⟶ read text and other course materials

go to class and take notes

read text and other course materials

review lecture notes

go to class and take notes

go to class and take notes

review lecture notes

read text and other course materials

The **Study Cycle** is a series of simple, yet important steps to implement throughout the semester *for each course.* Put these recommended steps into action starting with the first week of the term.

Keep in mind that descriptions of specific strategies for listening, taking notes, reading, and reviewing are provided in subsequent chapters.

1. **Go to class and take notes.** Take supplies—paper and pen, laptop, textbook, planner—and sit near the front. (Chapter 3 provides strategies for in-class note taking.)

    ⇩   ↖

    ⇩   ⇧

2. **Review your in-class notes** as soon as possible after class. Make⇧ time to organize, add to, and emphasize information within your notes. (See Chapter 3.)

    ⇩   ⇧

    ⇩   ⇧

3. **Read the assigned material** and create a study guide. (Chapter 2 provides detailed information about how to read, study, and learn from your textbook.)   ⇧

    ⇩

    ⇩   ⇧

4. **Go to class and take notes.** Be alert, ready to listen and write or type.   ⇧

    ⇩   ⇧

    ⇩

5. **Review your in-class notes** within 24 hours after class. Orga-⇧ nize, add to, emphasize, and summarize information within your notes.   ⇧

    ⇩

    ⇩   ⇧

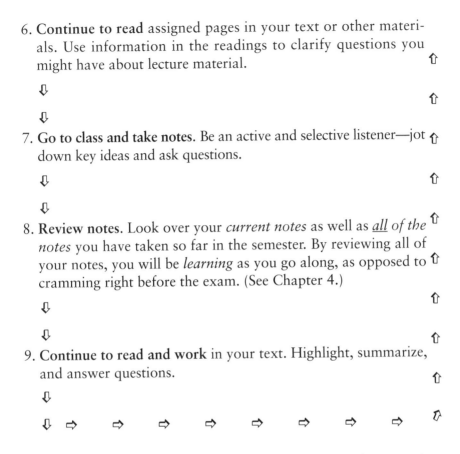

6. **Continue to read** assigned pages in your text or other materials. Use information in the readings to clarify questions you might have about lecture material.

7. **Go to class and take notes.** Be an active and selective listener—jot down key ideas and ask questions.

8. **Review notes.** Look over your *current notes* as well as <u>*all*</u> *of the notes* you have taken so far in the semester. By reviewing all of your notes, you will be *learning* as you go along, as opposed to cramming right before the exam. (See Chapter 4.)

9. **Continue to read and work** in your text. Highlight, summarize, and answer questions.

Repeat this cycle weekly throughout the semester. Notice how easy it is to spend 6 hours per week preparing and studying for each course! Bear in mind that by conscientiously applying these steps, you will be well on your way to excelling in your college coursework.

Three-Step Course of Action

In your Social Science course you likely are required to go beyond simple recall of information. To excel in the course you must obtain a deeper and more complex level of understanding of content. Learning strategies that assist you with acquiring this deeper understanding of Social Science content are described within each chapter of this handbook. The strategies are organized according to three steps: select, sort, and solidify.

1. **SELECT.** Begin with the question: ***What do I need to know for this course?*** To answer this question, you have to make decisions about what is important information for assignments, quizzes, tests, papers, and so on. You will be picking out key ideas as you read the text, listen in class, take notes, and study for exams.

2. **SORT.** In order to maximize your understanding, you need to <u>do</u> something with the key ideas you selected previously. For this step focus on the question: ***How can I summarize, organize, or personalize the information I need to know?*** To answer this question, you will employ strategies that help you clarify new and complex Social Science concepts, as well as make sense of the large amounts of material you will encounter.

3. **SOLIDIFY.** Besides understanding important content, you want to remember this information for an upcoming assignment, class discussion, or exam. For this step, consider the question: ***What can I do to retain information for future use?*** To answer this question, you will combine and reorganize ideas, review and reinforce key concepts, and consolidate material for future application.

The following chapters present specific strategies that guide you through this process of selecting, sorting, and solidifying information for your Social Science course. These strategies will maximize your learning as you proceed through the Study Cycle, that is; as you read your Social Science textbook, take notes and participate in class, and review and prepare for upcoming exams.

Student Comments

- As a freshman, I never paid attention to my course syllabi. As a result, I never knew what was due or what was happening in class. Now I look at the syllabus almost every day. It surprises me that I know so much more about what is going on in class!

  –Jacqui

- The Study Cycle helped me figure out what to do and how to study. In high school I never had to study, so when I started college I had no idea what to do outside of class.

  –Sam

2

READ THE TEXTBOOK

Importance of the Textbook

Your text is a valuable tool that helps you develop a thorough understanding of a Social Science course discipline. Some college instructors refer to the textbook regularly; others rarely mention the text or particular reading assignments. Either way, almost all college instructors assume that you are keeping up with reading the appropriate text chapters. Keep in mind that it is your responsibility to know what chapters and materials you should be reading for each course. Refer to the course syllabus regularly to keep track of assigned chapters, pages, and due dates. If the course syllabus does not contain specific reading assignments, look for the lecture topic on the syllabus. Then use the text index to find the corresponding pages to read.

Here are simple yet worthwhile suggestions for how to use your textbook before, during, and after class.

- **Before class.** Read—or at least skim—your text assignment before each class. Reading an assignment beforehand allows you to:
  - ◆ Become familiar with the topic, which prepares you to listen actively in class. Gaining even basic knowledge of a topic before a lecture will strengthen your understanding of in-class material.
  - ◆ Recognize names, terms, and other content-specific language that will be used in class.
  - ◆ Obtain a general idea of the organization of the material, which will strengthen the overall orderliness and clarity of the notes you take during class.

- **During class.** Have your textbook available during class.
  - If your instructor uses the text as a main source of information, highlight and write on chapter pages as your instructor talks.
  - Instructors often refer to illustrations and graphic materials in the text. Have those pages available to view during class.
  - When class material seems confusing and unclear, jot down the corresponding text pages. After class, reread those pages and add clarifying explanations and examples within your class notes.
  - If your instructor emphasizes particular text pages in class, make note of the pages. Your instructor considers this information to be important and, therefore, the information likely will be on an upcoming exam.
- **After class.** The textbook is a valuable tool after class when reviewing your lecture notes. As you go back through your class notes, refer to the text chapter in order to:
  - Fill in missing information and details in your notes.
  - Clarify confusing portions by adding explanations, examples, and application scenarios.
  - Deepen your understanding of a complex topic by reading multiple case studies and varied perspectives and analyses of the topic.

Characteristics of Social Science Textbooks

Certain characteristics are common to Social Science textbooks:

- **Content-specific vocabulary.** Knowledge of vocabulary is a foundation of understanding text material. Social Science text chapters tend to be full of terms common to the particular discipline. These terms may or may not be bolded, italicized, or defined. When reading, pay special attention to terms since they often are a significant part of class discussion, assignments, and exams.
- **Numerous names and dates.** Placing too much attention on the many names and dates in a chapter can make reading tedious and overwhelming. Instead, focus on main ideas, selecting only the names and dates that you likely need to know for an assignment or test.
- **Graphics.** Boxed inserts, pictures, charts, and graphs are interspersed within text pages. Graphics summarize large quantities

of information or difficult concepts, thus don't omit them when reading.

- **Examples and case studies.** Also, don't skip examples or case studies. These features help you to apply abstract information to concrete situations, making concepts and theories more relevant and understandable.
- **Text and chapter features.** Be aware of useful text features, including the table of contents, glossary, and index. In addition, utilize chapter features—such as learning objectives, list of terms, summary, and review questions—to familiarize yourself with content and organization before reading and to check your comprehension after reading.
- **Cause and effect connections.** As you read, pay attention to how one event or occurrence triggers another. In particular, focus on **watershed events;** that is, actions, experiences, or incidents that result in *significant changes*. Here are two examples of watershed events in recent history:

  I. Starting in 1989, three opposition groups challenged President Mikhail Gorbachev's leadership in the Soviet Union. ➔ In August 1991, attempted coup of Gorbachev by conservatives in government. ➔ Gorbachev under arrest. ➔ Coup collapsed. ➔ December 1991, Gorbachev relinquished his power. ➔ Commonwealth of Independent States formed. ➔ Official collapse of European communism in Soviet Union and Eastern Europe. *The attempted coup of Gorbachev followed by the relinquishing of his power was a watershed event because it resulted in the collapse of communism in a major world region.*

  II. Early 1970's, a woman raped in Texas. ➔ Two young lawyers challenged Texas law that abortion was criminal act. ➔ Legal case reached Supreme Court. ➔ Justices struck down Texas law as violation of a woman's right to reproductive privacy. *This case, Roe v. Wade, was a watershed event because it resulted in significant changes throughout the country in women's access to abortions.*

These Features Tend to be Unique in History Textbooks

- Sequential presentation of information.
- Long, uninterrupted passages, which can obscure main ideas.

- Densely written passages with each sentence containing important information.
- <u>Many</u> names and dates.
- Minimal text aids, with the exception of timelines that place key events in proper context.

How to Approach History Textbooks

Page 12 contains a passage from a 39-page chapter in an introductory-level History textbook. The passage is part of the first of five sections within the chapter. The chapter covers the years 1933–1945, the period leading up to and during World War II.

Look at the passage. Take note of these elements, which are typical of college-level History textbooks:

- The lack of bold print words, definitions, pictures, and illustrations.
- The compactness of the print and the lack of white spaces.
- The many dates.

Then examine the summary notes that a student jotted in the margins in order to better understand and remember information in this passage. The student followed this sequence before, during, and after reading the History text chapter:

Before

- Read the chapter outline in the detailed table of contents at the beginning of the text and on the first page of the chapter.
- Looked at the timeline at the beginning of the section. This helped to put chapter events into context.
- Turned chapter headings and sub-headings into questions, using open-ended question words: *what, why,* and *how.* Questions included:
  - *What were Hitler's goals?*
  - *How did Hitler plan to achieve his goals?*
  - *How did Germany rearm?*
  - *What was the League of Nations?*
  - *Why did the League of Nations fail?*

During

- Read the first paragraph twice since it was important yet confusing. Rereading the first paragraph set the stage for understanding the remainder of the section.
- In the section "Hitler's Goals," marked the goals and how Hitler intended to achieve them.
- In the section "Germany Rearms," marked signal words (*"The first problem," "At last"*) and intervening events. This helped him follow the sequence of ideas.
- Looked in the index to find more information about the League of Nations. Added information that helped him better understand this topic.

After

- Answered the questions formed before reading.
- Reviewed his text markings.
- Outlined information in the section in preparation for the lecture and an upcoming quiz.

Select, Sort, Solidify

Successfully reading and learning from a text doesn't just happen. Instead, you will need to plan strategically how you will understand and remember information within the text. These approaches will help you to read and study text material effectively and efficiently.

Strategies to SELECT Text Information

Before Reading

The following strategies help you answer the question: *What text material do I need to know for the upcoming assignment, quiz, or test?*

- *Identify your purpose for reading*. Knowing your purpose tends to increase both interest and concentration when reading. Clarify *why* you are reading the material, which can be one or more of the following reasons:
  - To gain basic background knowledge.
  - To prepare for class discussions.

(Continued)

AGAIN THE ROAD TO WAR (1933–1939)

World War I and the Versailles treaty had only a marginal relationship to the world depression of the 1930s. In Germany, however, where the reparations settlement had contributed to the vast inflation of 1923, economic and social discontent focused on the Versailles settlement as the cause of all ills. Throughout the late 1920s, Adolf Hitler and the Nazi Party denounced Versailles as the source of all of Germany's troubles. The economic woes of the early 1930s seemed to bear them out. Nationalism and attention to the social question, along with party discipline, had been the sources of Nazi success. They continued to influence Hitler's foreign policy after he became chancellor in January 1933. Moreover, the Nazi destruction of the Weimar constitution and of political opposition meant that Hitler himself totally dominated German foreign policy. Consequently, it is important to know what his goals were and how he planned to achieve them. *Germany: nationalism, unrest, strict rules*

HITLER'S GOALS ← *important!!*

From the first expression of his goals in a book written in jail, *Mein Kampf (My Struggle)*, to his last days in the underground bunker in Berlin where he killed himself, Hitler's racial theories and goals were at the center of his thought. He meant to go far beyond Germany's 1914 boundaries, which were the limit of the vision of his predecessors. He meant to bring the entire German people—the *Volk*—understood as a racial group, together into a single nation. *unite people* *acquire land*

The new Germany would include all the Germanic parts of the old Habsburg Empire, including Austria. This virile and growing nation would need more space to live, or *Lebensraum*, that would be taken from the Slavs, who, according to Nazi theory, were a lesser race, fit only for servitude. The removal of the Jews, another inferior race according to Nazi theory, would purify the new Germany. The plans required the conquest of Poland and Ukraine as the primary areas for German settlement and for providing badly needed food. Neither *Mein Kampf* nor later statements of policy were blueprints for action. Rather, Hitler was a brilliant improviser who exploited opportunities as they arose. He never lost sight of his goal, however, which would almost certainly require a *inferior races 1) Slavs 2) Jews*

major war. (See "Hitler Describes His Goals in Foreign Policy.")

Germany Rearms When Hitler came to power, Germany was far too weak to permit a direct approach to reach his aims. The first problem he set out to resolve was to shake off the fetters of Versailles and to make Germany a formidable military power. In October 1933, Germany withdrew from an international disarmament conference and also from the League of Nations. Hitler argued that because the other powers had not disarmed as they had promised, it was wrong to keep Germany helpless. These acts alarmed the French, but were merely symbolic. In January 1934, Germany signed a nonaggression pact with Poland that was of greater concern to France, for it undermined France's chief means of containing the Germans. At last, in March 1935, Hitler formally renounced the disarmament provisions of the Versailles treaty with the formation of a German air force, and soon he reinstated conscription, which aimed at an army of half a million men. *became military power* *left League of Nations* *no disarmament* *started draft*

The League of Nations Fails Growing evidence that the League of Nations could not keep the peace and that collective security was a myth made Hitler's path easier. In September 1931, Japan occupied Manchuria. China appealed to the League of Nations. The league dispatched a commission under a British diplomat, the earl of Lytton (1876–1951). The *Lytton Report* condemned the Japanese for resorting to force, but the powers were unwilling to impose sanctions. Japan withdrew from the League and kept control of Manchuria.

When Hitler announced his decision to rearm Germany, the League formally condemned that action, but it took no steps to prevent it. France and Britain felt unable to object forcefully because they had not carried out their own promises to disarm. Instead, they met with Mussolini in June 1935 to form the so-called Stresa Front, promising to use force to maintain the status quo in Europe. This show of unity was short lived, however. Britain, desperate to maintain superiority at sea, violated the spirit of the Stresa accords and sacrificed French security needs to make a separate naval agreement with Hitler. The pact allowed him to rebuild the German fleet to 35 percent of the British navy. Hitler had taken a major step toward his goal without provoking serious opposition. Italy's expansionist ambitions in Africa, however, soon brought it into conflict with the Western powers. *League didn't prevent German arming* *Britain naval agreement w/Hitler* *Hitler: no major objectors*

Source: Kagan, Donald; Ozment, Steven; Turner, Frank M., *Western Heritage: The Combined Volume*, 9th Edition, © 2007, p. 409. Reprinted by permission of Pearson Education, Inc., Upper Saddle River, NJ.

- To clarify material presented in class.
- To deepen your understanding.
- To learn information that will be on the exam.
- To use in a class assignment.

- *Review homework or notes from previous class.* This will help you put the new information in context of what your instructor is presenting in class.

- *Reduce distractions.* Minimizing external and internal distractions will maximize your concentration and alertness while reading.
  - Be rested, well-fed, and alert.
  - Move away from friends, TV, IM, and other outside sources of distractions.

- *Preview the chapter.* Flip through the pages and take note of:
  - The main topics.
  - How information is organized.
  - Pictures, graphics, bold print, italicized words, and other visual aids. Look at these before you read so that they don't disrupt your concentration while you are reading.
  - Key terms. Look up terms you don't understand; write definitions in the margins or on index cards.
  - Introductions, summaries, and chapter questions.
  - Overall difficulty level of the material.

Student Comments

- A reading plan helps me manage my time so that I finish each reading assignment. My Sociology textbook has long chapters. I first look at the whole chapter and write down the amount of time I need to read. So far I am getting each chapter read on time.

  –Kylie

- A strategy I use is to look at bold headings and important words before reading. This helps me know what I have to focus on as I read.

  –Ana

Strategies to SORT Text Information
During Reading
Employ strategies that help you clarify and understand text material. Answer the question: *How can I summarize, organize, or personalize text information that I need to know?*

- *Break up reading into logical segments.* Concentrate on one section of the chapter at a time.
- *Turn section headings into questions.* Read to discover answers to your questions. Use the words "what," "how," or "why" when formulating questions. For example: *What are key characteristics of Social Science texts? How do I know what text material is important? Why should I preview a chapter?*
- *Mark, write, and highlight in your book.*
  - ◆ Highlight or underline important terms or phrases. Be careful to identify just the main points, that is, highlight no more than 20% of a text page.
  - ◆ Use margins to paraphrase and summarize key ideas.
  - ◆ Add numbers to call attention to the order of ideas.
  - ◆ Use color and symbols to emphasize importance.
- *Pay special attention to examples, illustrations, and graphics.* These features will help you understand important concepts.
- *Recite aloud.* After reading a section, look away and restate key information *in your own words.* If you can't do it, read the section again!
- *Make personal connections.* Add your own examples. Link text information with real-life situations.
- *Refer back to your lecture notes* when reading after a class. Focus on how the text and class information fit together. Clarify your class notes by adding information from your text.
- *Take periodic breaks.* Afterward, *review the previous section* before starting to read the next.

Strategies to SOLIDIFY Text Information
After Reading
You want to maximize your ability to remember important text material. Employ strategies that answer the question: *What can I do to retain text information for future use?*

- *Review the chapter.*
  - Reread your marginal notes.
  - Answer beginning-of-chapter learning objectives or focus questions. In your own words, answer end-of-chapter comprehension questions.
  - Define and give examples for important terms and concepts. Know *who* key people are and *why* they are important.
- *Develop a study guide.* Condense and summarize important text information. You can utilize a variety of formats:
  - Review charts and timelines.
  - Concept or mind maps.
  - Questions and answers.
  - Summary outlines.
  - Study cards.
- *Recite aloud.* As you review, talk aloud to yourself in order to provide auditory reinforcement of important information.

Student Comments

- I use textbook marking for most of my assignments. Marking text pages helps with my comprehension and retention because it makes me read more in depth. I jot down a note or two about what I just read, and then move on to the next paragraph. It's extremely helpful to me in Psychology, which requires a lot of reading.

–Jen

Example of Textbook Marking

A student followed this sequence when reading the section, "Classical Conditioning," (see following pages) in the Psychology textbook.

CHAPTER 6 LEARNING

Classical Conditioning

The story of habituation could hardly be more straightforward. We experience a stimulus, respond to it, and then stop responding after repeated exposure. We've learned something significant, but we haven't learned to forge connections between two stimuli. Yet a great deal of learning depends on associating one thing with another. If we never learned to connect one stimulus, like the appearance of an apple, with another stimulus, like its taste, our world would remain what William James (1891) called a "blooming, buzzing confusion"—a world of disconnected sensory experiences.

BRITISH ASSOCIATIONISM

Knowledge = connecting stimuli

Several centuries ago, a school of thinkers called the *British Associationists* believed that we acquire virtually all of our knowledge by connecting one stimulus with another: the sound of our mother's voice with her face, for example. Once we form these associations, we need only recall one element of the pair to retrieve the other. Even thinking about a sensation often triggers it. For example, as you read about your mother's face, you might have pictured her in your mind. The British Associationists, who included David Hartley (1707–1757) and John Stuart Mill (1806–1873), believed that simple associations provided the mental building blocks for more complex ideas. Your understanding of this paragraph, they surely would have suggested, stems from thousands of linkages you've formed between the words in it—like *sound* and *voice*—and other words, which are in turn linked to simple concepts, which are in turn linked to more complex concepts . . . and, well, you get the picture.

PAVLOV'S DISCOVERIES

The Rolling Stones may be the only major rock band to accurately describe the process of classical conditioning. One of their well-known songs refers to a man salivating like one of Pavlov's dogs whenever the object of his affection calls his name. Not bad for a group of non-psychologists!

The history of science teaches us that many discoveries arise from *serendipity*, or accident. Yet it takes a great scientist to capitalize on serendipitous observations that others regard as meaningless flukes. As French microbiologist Louis Pasteur, who discovered the process of pasteurizing milk, observed, "Chance favors the prepared mind." So it was with the discoveries of Russian scientist Ivan Pavlov. His landmark understanding of classical conditioning emerged from a set of unforeseen observations that were unrelated to his main research interests.

Pavlov - initial research in digestion

Pavlov's primary research was digestion in dogs—in fact, his discoveries concerning digestion, not classical conditioning, earned him the Nobel Prize in 1904. Pavlov placed dogs in a harness and inserted a *cannula*, or collection tube, into their salivary glands to study their salivary responses to meat powder. In doing so, he observed something unexpected: He found that dogs began salivating not only to the meat powder itself, but to previously neutral stimuli that had become associated with it, such as research assistants who brought in the powder. Indeed, the dogs even salivated to the sound of these assistants' footsteps as they approached the laboratory. The dogs seemed to be anticipating the meat powder and responding to stimuli that signaled its arrival.

dogs salivate at SIGNAL of food

We call this process of association **classical conditioning** (or **Pavlovian** or **respondent conditioning**): a form of learning in which animals come to respond to a previously neutral stimulus that had been paired with another stimulus that elicits an automatic response. Yet Pavlov's initial observations were merely anecdotal, so like any good scientist he put his informal observations to a more rigorous test.

classical (Pavlovian or respondent) conditioning
form of learning in which animals come to respond to a previously neutral stimulus that had been paired with another stimulus that elicits an automatic response

conditioned stimulus (CS)
initially neutral stimulus

THE CLASSICAL CONDITIONING PHENOMENON *know this!*

Here's how Pavlov first demonstrated classical conditioning systematically (see **Figure 6.2**).

(1) He started with an initially neutral stimulus, called the **conditioned stimulus (CS)**. In this case, Pavlov used a metronome, a clicking pendulum that keeps time (in other studies, Pavlov used a tuning fork or whistle; contrary to urban legend, Pavlov didn't use a bell). This stimulus doesn't elicit much, if any, response from the dogs. Interestingly, the term

CS

Figure 6.2 Pavlov's Classical Conditioning Model. UCS (meat powder) is paired with CS (metronome clicking) and produces UCR (salivation). Then CS is presented alone, and CR (salivation) occurs.

conditioned stimulus is apparently a mistranslation from the original Russian. Pavlov actually referred to it as the *conditional* stimulus, because the animal's response to it is conditional—that is, dependent—on learning. ★

(2) He then paired the CS again and again with an **unconditioned stimulus (UCS)**. (This term was *unconditional stimulus* in the original Russian, because the animal responds to it unconditionally, that is, all of the time or automatically.) In the case of Pavlov's dogs, the UCS was the meat powder. The UCS elicits an automatic, reflexive response called the **unconditioned response (UCR)**, in this case salivation. The key point is that the animal doesn't need to learn to respond to the UCS with the UCR. It produces the UCR without any training at all, because the response is a product of nature, not nurture.

UCS causes UCR

(3) Pavlov repeatedly paired the CS and UCS—and observed something remarkable. If he now presented the CS (the metronome) alone, it elicited a response, namely, salivation. This new response is the **conditioned response (CR)**: a response previously associated with a nonneutral stimulus that comes to be elicited by a neutral stimulus. Lo and behold, learning has occurred. ★ The dog, which previously did nothing when it heard the metronome except perhaps turn its head toward it, now salivates when it hears the metronome. The CR, in contrast to the UCR, is a product of nurture, not nature.

← CR   *product of nurture*

In most cases, the CR is similar to the UCR but it's rarely identical to it. For example, Pavlov found that dogs salivated less in response to the metronome (the CS) than to the meat powder (the UCS).

see class notes

CS + UCS > UCR
CS > UCR > CR

Few findings in psychology are as replicable as classical conditioning. We can apply the classical conditioning paradigm to just about any animal with an intact nervous system, and demonstrate it repeatedly without fail. If only all psychological findings were so dependable!

Replicability

AVERSIVE CONDITIONING

We can classically condition organisms not only to positive UCSs, like food, but to negative UCSs, like stimuli inducing pain or nausea. If you were allergic to daisies and sneezed uncontrollably whenever you were near them—whether you saw them or not—you'd probably develop an automatic avoidance response, like shying away from a bouquet even before you realized why you were doing it. This type of avoidance response reflects *aversive conditioning*: classical conditioning to an unpleasant UCS (Emmelkamp & Kamphuis, 2005). Stanley Kubrick's 1971 film *A Clockwork Orange* provides an unforgettable example of aversive conditioning involving the main character, Alexander de Large, portrayed by actor Malcolm McDowell. De Large's prison captors, who hoped to eradicate his bloodthirsty lust for violence, forced him to watch film clips of aggressive individuals, like the members of Hitler's army marching in unison, while experiencing nausea induced by injections of a serum. The aversive conditioning worked—but only for a while.

negative UCR causes avoidance

factoid

Classical conditioning may occur not only in animals but in plants. One researcher found that a *Mimosa* plant that folds its leaves (UCR) when touched (UCS) can be conditioned to fold its leaves (CR) in response to a change in lighting condition (CS) that has been repeatedly paired with a touch (Haney, 1969). Nevertheless, this finding is scientifically controversial.

unconditioned stimulus (UCS)
stimulus that elicits an automatic response

unconditioned response (UCR)
automatic response to a nonneutral stimulus that does not need to be learned

conditioned response (CR)
response previously associated with a nonneutral stimulus that is elicited by a neutral stimulus through conditioning

Source: From Lilienfeld, Scott O., et al. *Psychology: From Inquiry to Understanding*, 1st Edition. Published by Allyn and Bacon, Boston, MA Copyright © 2009 by Pearson Education. Reprinted by permission of the publisher.

Select

- Previewed the section; looked at headings, bold print, illustrations, and marginal notes.
- Formed a general idea of the type of information presented. Realized the topic was complicated, with confusing terms (i.e. *conditioned* vs. *unconditioned, stimulus* vs. *response*).

Sort

- Read first subsection "British Associationism." Stopped and thought about what was important to know.
- Wrote a brief marginal note that summarized a point.
- Read second subsection "Pavlov's Discoveries." Decided to highlight key words that defined bold-faced terms. Also, added brief marginal notations that summarized and emphasized key ideas.
- Repeated process for remaining subsections.
- Used abbreviations and symbols ("→" = connection; "*" = important).
- Circled a phrase she did not understand. Wrote a reminder to check class notes for more explanations.
- Looked for associations between the text and what she already knew. Realized she needed more examples.

Solidify

- Reviewed her text notes the following day.
- Participated in the weekly group review session the following evening. Worked on creating examples of classical conditioning.
- Looked over text and notes before next class session.

Examples of Study Guides

Timeline for History Text Chapter

A student followed this sequence when previewing and reading the History chapter:

Select

- Looked at syllabus—a 50-point multiple choice chapter test was scheduled for the next week.
- Previewed the chapter. Realized the information was presented sequentially, building up to the Holocaust and ending with the creation of Israel.
- Noted particular names and terms (many of which were bold-faced in the text) which likely he needed to know. Used these dates, names, and terms to guide his reading and answer the question: *What do I need to know for this course?*

Sort

- After reading each section, wrote dates in the margin and highlighted key names and terms associated with each date.
- Added information in the margins that he remembered hearing from his grandfather, who served in the army during WWII.

Solidify

- Created a timeline summarizing key points (below). Wrote dates on left side of the paper, jotted down key points, then highlighted important terms and names.
- Used the study guide to review the chapter material: (1) Covered one side of the paper and quizzed himself. (2) Focused on explanations for highlighted words. (3) Cut the events side of the chart into strips and re-organized the events without looking at dates.

Holocaust Timeline

1920	Nazi Party formed.
1929	Heinrich **Himmler** was appointed head of the **SS**, Hitler's elite guard known for brutality.

(Continued)

Holocaust Timeline *(Continued)*

1930s	*Hitler Jugend*—Hitler Youth—was established to spread anti-Semitic and nationalistic propaganda to young boys.
1933	Hitler became Chancellor on January 30.
1933	*Enabling Act* gave Hitler total dictatorial power for four years.
1933–38	Nazis boycotted Jewish businesses; forbade intermarriage between Jews and Germans.
1933	Joseph **Goebbels** appointed minister of propaganda for the Nazi party.
1933	Nazis built first concentration camps in Germany, modeled after Native American reservations in the U.S.
1934	Adolf Hitler became *der Fuhrer*, or leader, of Germany after the death of Hindenburg.
1935	*Nuremberg Racial Laws* deprived German Jews of their citizenship.
1937	*Buchenwald* concentration camp established in Germany. Notorious for medical experiments—amputations, lethal germs, & poisons—performed on human subjects.
1938	*Anschluss*—Germany invaded Austria, though invasion is portrayed as a union.
1938	*Kristallnacht*—Jewish property was attacked in Germany on the "night of broken glass."
1939	World War II officially began with declaration of war on Germany by Britain and France.
1939	*Blitzpogrom*—three million Polish Jews were subjected to rape and murder.
1941	United States entered war as a result of **Pearl Harbor**.
1942	Hitler proposed the **Final Solution** of the "Jewish problem"; the Holocaust truly begins.
1943	**Warsaw Uprising**—Ghetto uprising by Jews.
1945	Advancing Allied Armies discover Nazi extermination camps; 6 million Jews murdered.
1948	Creation of the nation Israel.

Question-and-Answer Study Guide for Psychology Text

A student followed this sequence as she previewed and read the section in the Psychology text:

Select

- Determined that the instructor would lecture on Classical Conditioning in class.
- Previewed the section by looking at headings, bold print, and illustrations.
- Turned each heading into a question, writing on notebook paper (below).

Sort

- Read each subsection, then stopped to answer the question. If could not answer, reread.
- Answered each question in own words; wrote answer below the question, underlining some key words (below).
- Changed or expanded question to fit content, as needed.

Solidify

- After reading, went back and recited the answers without looking at notes.
- Checked each answer before moving on to the next question.

Question: *What is Classical Conditioning?*
Answer: Subjects taught automatic responses to new stimulus after frequent pairing of new + initial stimulus. Has these factors:

- Conditioned Stimulus (CS) – Subject has no response to CS at start of experiment. Response dependent on learning.

(Continued)

- Unconditioned Stimulus (UCS) – What the subject responds to (ex: food).
- Unconditioned Response (UCR) – Automatic, reflexive response (ex: saliva).
- Conditioned Response (CR) – Same response as UCR, but happens w/o food, just to CS.

Question: *Who discovered Classical Conditioning?*
Answer: Ivan Pavlov.
Question: *What is British Associationism?*
Answer: Developed idea that knowledge made by connecting stimuli. Students recall information by remembering one stimulus which leads to another. Thousands of connections needed for complex knowledge.
Question: *How did Pavlov discover Classical Conditioning?*
Answer: Researched digestion initially. Noticed that, before actually tasting powder, dogs would salivate at sound of research assistants bringing meat powder.
Question: *What is Aversive Conditioning?*
Answer: Subject presented with something negative, like pain (UCS) paired with something they want to avoid, like smoking. Then begin to associate negative UCS with what they want to avoid. Used to train subjects to avoid certain activities or stimuli.

Summary Chart

The chart is an overview of text strategies presented in this chapter. Use the chart as you plan approaches for reading and studying content in your Social Science course.

SELECT	SORT	SOLIDIFY
BEFORE:	DURING:	AFTER:

✓ Know your purpose for reading.
✓ Review homework or notes from the previous class.
✓ Reduce distractions.
✓ Preview the chapter.
	✓ Turn section headings into questions. Read to discover answers.
	✓ Mark, write, and highlight in your book.
	✓ Pay attention to examples, illustrations, and graphics.
	✓ Recite aloud.
	✓ Make personal connections.
	✓ Refer back to class notes.
	✓ Review previous section.
		✓ Review the chapter:
		  o Marginal notes.
		  o Chapter questions.
		  o Key terms, concepts, and people.
		✓ Develop a study guide:
		  o Review charts and timelines.
		  o Concept or mind maps.
		  o Questions and answers.
		  o Summary outlines.
		  o Study cards.
		✓ Recite aloud.

Student Comments

- I use textbook markings in my Anthropology class because my instructor teaches mainly from the book. Also, I use concept maps to link what I am reading. Concept maps help me combine my thoughts with the new ideas that I am learning.

  –José

- Graphic organizers help me a lot. I'm an artistic and visual learner, so I use many charts, outlines, and diagrams that show relationships between the information I'm reading.

  –Terrell

Text Strategies: Taking Action

Take time to stop, reflect, and apply the information presented in this chapter. Follow these five steps, using the sheets on the subsequent pages:

1. Identify a current reading assignment for your Social Science course. Fill in course name, the chapter or pages, and due date.

2. Place a check next to the strategies you will use for this assignment. You should do *all* of the four strategies from the **SELECT** column, *at least three* of the seven strategies from the **SORT** column, and *at least one* of the three strategies from the **SOLIDIFY** column.

3. Cut out the strip. Use it as a bookmark to remind you of your reading plan.

4. Afterward, take a moment to evaluate your success.

5. Repeat these steps for your next reading assignment, using another sheet. Build on previous approaches that worked for you.

Course: Chapter or pages: Due date:

SELECT	SORT	SOLIDIFY
BEFORE:	DURING:	AFTER:
___Know your purpose for reading.	___Turn section headings into questions. Read to discover answers.	___Review the chapter:
___Review home-work or notes from the previous class.	___Mark, write, and highlight in your book.	o Marginal notes.
___Reduce distractions.	___Pay attention to examples, illustrations, and graphics.	o Chapter questions.
___Preview the chapter.	___Recite aloud.	o Key terms, concepts, and people.
	___Make personal connections.	___Develop a study guide:
	___Refer back to class notes.	o Review charts and timelines.
	___Review previous section.	o Concept or mind maps.
		o Questions and answers.
		o Summary out-lines.
		o Study cards.
		___Recite aloud.

Evaluate Your Success: *For this assignment, which strategies helped you to understand and remember information? Highlight or circle each strategy that assisted you with reading and studying more effectively.*

Course: Chapter or pages: Due date:

SELECT	SORT	SOLIDIFY

BEFORE:

___Know your purpose for reading.

___Review homework or notes from the previous class.

___Reduce distractions.

___Preview the chapter.

DURING:

___Turn section headings into questions. Read to discover answers.

___Mark, write, and highlight in your book.

___Pay attention to examples, illustrations, and graphics.

___Recite aloud.

___Make personal connections.

___Refer back to class notes.

___Review previous section.

AFTER:

___Review the chapter:
- o Marginal notes.
- o Chapter questions.
- o Key terms, concepts, and people.

___Develop a study guide:
- o Review charts and timelines.
- o Concept or mind maps.
- o Questions and answers.
- o Summary outlines.
- o Study cards.

___Recite aloud.

Evaluate Your Success: *For this assignment, which strategies helped you to understand and remember information? Highlight or circle each strategy that assisted you with reading and studying more effectively.*

3

TAKE IN-CLASS NOTES

Importance of Taking Notes in Class

Be prepared to take notes in *each* class session. Whatever the class format—be it conventional lecture, guest speaker, video or movie, or group presentation—be ready to listen attentively and take notes. Subject matter covered in class is a summary of what your instructor has identified as significant within the Social Science discipline and, therefore, the information likely will appear on an upcoming test. The majority of questions on exams in lower-level Social Science courses tend to come from materials covered during class time. Note taking, either on paper or with a computer, is a vital aspect of identifying and understanding important information presented in class.

Format of Class Notes

Most Social Science classes encompass one or more of the following formats for class notes.

- **Traditional lecture notes**. In more conventional classes, the instructor talks during most of class time. Students are expected to write or type a summary of the content presented by the instructor. Topics presented in class often parallel content in a textbook or other reading assignment. During class the instructor sometimes asks questions to spark student input or includes activities to reinforce important concepts.
- **Web-based notes**. Many instructors place lecture notes on a Web-based program. If you are in this situation, *do* preview the notes

before each class. Bring the notes to class, either hard copies or on your laptop. Refer to these notes throughout the class session, adding to the information that is discussed, highlighting ideas that are emphasized, and jotting references to text pages and other readings.

- **PowerPoint® notes.** Many instructors use Microsoft PowerPoint presentations in class. Most PowerPoint slides are a bare-bones listing of topics; therefore, it is important that you add explanations, examples, and other details during class. If the PowerPoint slides are available beforehand, print them out and write on the hard copies, adding and highlighting information discussed during the class session.

- **Skeleton notes.** At times an instructor provides a skeleton outline of lecture notes which students can purchase from a copy center or print from the Internet. These notes contain only main topics with plenty of white space for students to add details, examples, and further explanations.

- **Audio notes.** Increasingly instructors make lecture material available to download on an MP3 player or computer, especially in large lecture classes. If you are ill and cannot attend class, use the podcast or audio material to keep abreast of lecture material. Also, listen to the audio content when doing other activities—such as walking, exercising, or laundry—in order to review and reinforce lecture material. However, do not rely on a podcast or audio material to replace regular class attendance. You are more likely to pay closer attention when listening and taking notes in the classroom. Furthermore, you will pick up helpful cues when in the same room as the instructor and other students.

A common characteristic of all five formats of class notes is the need for students to actively listen and decide what information *is* or *is not* important. If you think material is important—write it down. If you are not sure if an idea is important—write it down, also. Since you will be taking time after class to review and edit your notes, it is best to err on the side of including extra ideas, as opposed to too few ideas. Note taking during class is part of active decision making, that is, selecting, sorting, and solidifying Social Science content. No matter what the format, the following strategies will maximize your ability to understand and remember in-class material.

Select, Sort, Solidify

Importantly, *go to every class*. As mentioned previously, you are more likely to create clear, understandable notes when you are sitting in the classroom, as opposed to listening only to a podcast or copying another student's notes. The following strategies will assist you to listen actively and take notes that enhance your understanding and remembering of class content.

Strategies to SELECT In-Class Material

Begin by deciding what information is important. Answer the question: *What in-class material do I need to know for the upcoming assignment, quiz, or test?*

Before Class

Obtain background and familiarity with topics to be discussed in class:

- **Review information on the course syllabus.** Notice which topics will be covered during the class session.
- **Skim homework and notes from the previous class.** This will focus your attention and prepare you to listen.
- **Skim the corresponding text chapter.** Quickly read the introduction and summary, headings and subheadings, bold-faced and italicized words, and graphic features. For a more thorough background and deeper understanding, read the entire chapter.
- **Obtain online notes.** Make online notes available to use during class by either printing out hard copies or bringing your laptop.

During Class

- **Sit in middle-front of the classroom.** You will see and hear more clearly and minimize surrounding distractions, especially in large auditorium-style classrooms.
- **Listen selectively—focus on ideas** (as opposed to words). Concentrate on:
  - *Main ideas* about the topic.
  - *Explanations, details, and examples* that support each main idea.
  - *Relationships or connections* among the ideas. Your notes should reflect how ideas are related or organized. Here are six common ways ideas are presented in the content of a lecture:

- **Definitions.** Content includes either a formal or informal meaning of terms or concepts. In your notes, paraphrase the definitions, adding explanations and examples.
- **Examples.** Content includes illustrations that describe, explain, and/or personalize important terms or concepts. In your notes, leave space to add your own examples after class.
- **Cause and effect.** Content includes how an idea or event triggers another. In your notes, make sure this cause/effect connection is obvious.
- **Order.** Content presented as an order of importance or a time order. In your notes, use numbers (1, 2, 3 . . .) to emphasize the order of ideas or steps in a sequence.
- **Compare and contrast.** Content presents similarities and differences among ideas. After class, summarize the information by creating a chart, with one column listing similarities and the other listing differences.
- **Rationale.** Content provides details that clarify the reasons *why* something happened. In your notes, provide clear, concrete, and substantial explanations.

- **Be attentive of verbal cues.** Every instructor provides verbal cues, or signals, indicating the importance of particular information. For example, an instructor asks questions, repeats or paraphrases information, or talks louder or slower. If your instructor emphasizes an idea, include it in your notes!
- **Be attentive of non-verbal cues.** Likewise, be aware of your instructor's behaviors and mannerisms that indicate ideas are important. For example, an instructor writes on the board, uses hand gestures, paces, or makes eye contact.
- **Use phrases, abbreviations, and symbols.** Often speed is a factor when taking notes in class. Therefore, eliminate unnecessary words—write in phrases and not whole sentences. Also, eliminate unnecessary letters—use abbreviations and symbols.
- **Utilize Web notes.** On your Web notes, highlight ideas that the instructor emphasizes. In addition, add details and examples that help to explain information.
- **Ask questions.** Let the instructor know if you are confused or uncertain about content. Ask questions to clarify information and help you stay alert during class time.

Strategies to SORT In-Class Material

Employ strategies that help you clarify and understand in-class material. Answer the question: *How can I summarize, organize, or personalize in-class information that I need to know?*

After Class

- **Review notes soon after each class.** Within 24 hours after class, take the time to look over your notes and check for understanding.
- **Make additions or changes,** as needed, to clarify information in your notes.
  - ◆ *Organize* ideas.
  - ◆ *Paraphrase* ideas in your own words.
  - ◆ *Add* examples and explanations.
  - ◆ *Fill in* text information.
  - ◆ *Highlight* or *underline* key terms and concepts.
- **Think about upcoming tests.** Identify broad ideas and concepts which are potential essay questions. Look for individual items and details which might be short answer questions. Also, recognize potential case study and application questions.

Strategies to SOLIDIFY In-Class Material

Employ strategies that maximize your ability to remember in-class material. Answer the question: *What can I do to retain in-class information for future use?*

After Class

- **Review weekly.** Set aside a block of time (such as Sunday evening) to go back through your in-class notes. Note the continuation and transition of ideas and how topics relate to each other.
- **Participate in study/review sessions.** Ask and answer questions with other classmates.
- **Make sample test questions** from your notes.
- **Recite aloud.** As you review, talk aloud to yourself to provide auditory reinforcement.

Student Comments

- When I review my notes after each class I notice that I am better prepared for the next class and am able to follow the instructor's lectures much more easily.

  —Taurena

- My instructor posts her lecture notes online. I print out the notes before class and read over them. When I print them out I change them to double spaced, so that in class I can add examples and other information from the instructor.

  —Chris

- In Art History, I was so uninterested and was struggling to stay awake during class. I forced myself to become interested. I started looking at the architecture on campus, went to gallery exhibits, and even talked to other people about what I was learning. Now I find myself genuinely interested in the subject and am able to grasp more in class. Sitting through an hour and a half of lecture has become a lot easier.

  —Amiel

Examples of Notes

Notes from Sociology Class

A student followed this sequence before, during, and after class (see her notes on the following page):

Sort

- Before class, reviewed the syllabus and saw that the instructor would start a new chapter.
- Skimmed the chapter. Noted the title, overview, color-coded headings and sub-headings, abundance of illustrations, reading tips, and sample test questions.
- At start of class, headed the notepaper with date, chapter title, and topic written on the board.
- As instructor spoke, focused on writing main ideas and key terms, with supporting explanations and examples underneath.

(Continued)

- Left spaces between topics. Used phrases, abbreviations, and symbols.
- Asked the instructor a question about "social vs. biological differences." Wrote down the example that the instructor provided.

Select

- That evening, went back through the in-class notes. Highlighted key words; added summary (**Each had . . .**), text reference (**see p. 331**), and emphasis (**def., know . . .**).

Solidify

- Each Monday morning, reviewed consecutive Sociology class notes. Wrote down questions for weekly study group.

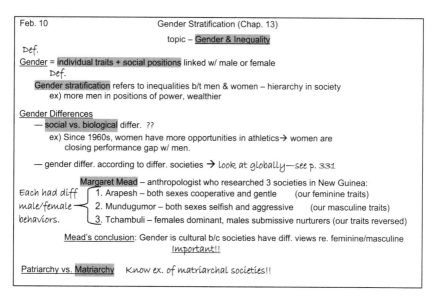

```
Feb. 10                    Gender Stratification (Chap. 13)
                              topic – Gender & Inequality
     Def.
Gender = individual traits + social positions linked w/ male or female
          Def.
     Gender stratification refers to inequalities b/t men & women – hierarchy in society
          ex) more men in positions of power, wealthier

Gender Differences
     — social vs. biological differ.  ??
          ex) Since 1960s, women have more opportunities in athletics→ women are
               closing performance gap w/ men.

     — gender differ. according to differ. societies  → look at globally—see p. 331

                Margaret Mead – anthropologist who researched 3 societies in New Guinea:
Each had diff   ┌ 1. Arapesh – both sexes cooperative and gentle      (our feminine traits)
male/female ──┤   2. Mundugumor – both sexes selfish and aggressive    (our masculine traits)
behaviors.      └ 3. Tchambuli – females dominant, males submissive nurturers (our traits reversed)

          Mead's conclusion: Gender is cultural b/c societies have diff. views re. feminine/masculine
                              Important!!

     Patriarchy vs. Matriarchy   Know ex. of matriarchal societies!!
```

Based on: Macionis, J. J. (2008). *Sociology*, 12th Edition, Chapter 13, Gender Stratification, p. 329–355. Published by Pearson Prentice Hall, Upper Saddle River, NJ.

Web Notes from Political Science Class

A student followed this sequence before, during, and after class:

Sort

- Before class, downloaded that day's notes (see following page), in outline format, onto his laptop computer. Previewed the outline—the right column was empty in order for students to add information from class and textbook.
- Skimmed Chapter 15. Was struck by the length (40 pages) and density of the material. Decided to allow lots of time after class to read and add text information.
- During class, highlighted terms and information that the instructor emphasized. In the right column, typed in additional explanations and examples derived from class discussion.

Select

- Set aside blocks of study time that evening and the following afternoon. As he read a section of the chapter, he reviewed the corresponding material within his class notes.
- Added text information in the right column of the notes.

Solidify

- Referred to notes when completing the 20-question Chapter Review Test.
- Reviewed class and text material out loud with two classmates each Monday evening. Focused on answering the end-of-chapter Discussion Questions since the test will consist of essay questions.

Date: **October 24**	Topic: **Political Parties**	Text Chapter: **15**
I. Major political parties as "umbrella" organizations.		Umbrella means includes a range of issues, coalitions, & interest groups.
II. Religion and Political Parties.		
A. First Amendment: separation of state & church.		Citizens free to practice any religion, but gov't cannot establish a religion -- p. 579
B. Merging of religion & politics.		
1. 1980s: influence of evangelical Christians.		called the Religious Right
2. grassroots networking.		
3. Christian Coalition partnered with Republican Party.		p. 580-1: example in Missouri
4. 1994: Republicans voted into office at all levels.		**influx of CC into politics produced Republican majority w/ conservative agenda
III. Models of Political Parties.		
A. Pragmatic party model: sponsor candidates to control government.		know difference b/t models
B. Responsible party model: sponsor candidates to shape public policy.		
C. Characteristics of Political Parties.		vs. Interest Groups
1. Nominate candidates under own label.		1. don't nominate
2. Have party platform with wide range of policy positions.		2. narrow range of issues
3. Subject to state and local laws.		3. private organizations—no gov't. rules

Based on: Shea, D. M., Green, J. C., & Smith, C. E. (2007). *Living Democracy,* National ed., Chapter 15, Political Parties, p. 579–619. Published by Pearson Prentice Hall, Upper Saddle River, NJ.

Summary Chart

This is an overview of note-taking strategies presented in the chapter. Use the chart as you plan approaches for listening and taking notes in your Social Science course.

SELECT	SORT	SOLIDIFY
BEFORE:	AFTER:	AFTER:
✓ Review syllabus.	✓ Review notes soon after class.	✓ Review weekly.
✓ Skim homework and previous notes.	✓ Make additions or changes to clarify information.	✓ Participate in study/review sessions.
✓ Skim related text chapter.	o Organize ideas.	✓ Make sample test questions.
✓ Have online notes ready.	o Add examples and explanations.	✓ Recite aloud.

SELECT*(Continued)*	SORT *(Continued)*
DURING:	AFTER: *(Continued)*
✓ Sit in middle-front of the classroom.	o Fill in text information.
✓ Listen selectively; focus on ideas.	o Highlight or underline key terms and concepts.
✓ Be attentive of verbal and non-verbal cues.	
✓ Use phrases, abbreviations, and symbols in notes.	
✓ Utilize Web notes.	
✓ Ask questions.	

Student Comments

- My Political Science instructor is very unorganized—I cannot follow his lectures. I have to rewrite my notes after class and follow the organization in the class textbook.

  —Yoshi

- I used to view each day's notes as separate entities. Then I started looking for patterns and soon was able to associate the topics from one lecture to the next. Now I understand more and am more interested in what my professor is saying!

  —Marta

Note-Taking Strategies: Taking Action

Reflect on and apply information presented in this chapter. Follow these five steps, using sheets on the subsequent pages:

1. Fill in the name of your Social Science course, date of the class session, and topic covered.
2. Place a check next to the strategies you will use for this class.
   - ◆ In the **SELECT** column, choose *at least two* of the four strategies to do BEFORE class and *at least two* of the six strategies to do DURING class.

- ◆ In the **SORT** column, choose *at least one* of the two strategies to do AFTER class.
- ◆ In the **SOLIDIFY** column, choose *at least two* of the four strategies to do AFTER class.

3. Cut out the sheet. As a reminder, place it in your notebook or post it on your computer.

4. Afterward, take a moment to evaluate your success.

5. Repeat these steps for another class session, building on approaches that have worked.

Course: Date: Topic:

SELECT	SORT	SOLIDIFY
BEFORE:	AFTER:	AFTER:
___Review syllabus.	___Review notes	___Review weekly.
___Skim homework	soon after class.	___Participate in
and previous	___Make additions	study/review
notes.	or changes to	sessions.
___Skim related	clarify	___Make sample
text chapter.	information.	test questions.
___Have online	o Organize ideas.	___Recite aloud.
notes ready.	o Add examples	
	and explana-	
DURING:	tions.	
___Sit in middle-	o Fill in text	
front of the	information.	
classroom.	o Highlight or	
___Listen selectively;	underline	
focus on ideas.	key terms	
___Be attentive of	and concepts.	
verbal and non-		
verbal cues.		
___Use phrases,		
abbreviations,		
and symbols in		
notes.		
___Utilize Web		
notes.		
___Ask questions.		

Evaluate Your Success: *Highlight or circle each strategy that assisted you to listen and take notes more effectively.*

Course: Date: Topic:

SELECT	SORT	SOLIDIFY
BEFORE:	AFTER:	AFTER:
___Review syllabus.	___Review notes soon after class.	___Review weekly.
___Skim homework and previous notes.	___Make additions or changes to clarify information.	___Participate in study/review sessions.
___Skim related text chapter.	o Organize ideas.	___Make sample test questions.
___Have online notes ready.	o Add examples and explanations.	___Recite aloud.
DURING:	o Fill in text information.	
___Sit in middle-front of the classroom.	o Highlight or underline key terms and concepts.	
___Listen selectively; focus on ideas.		
___Be attentive of verbal and non-verbal cues.		
___Use phrases, abbreviations, and symbols in notes.		
___Utilize Web notes.		
___Ask questions.		

Evaluate Your Success: *Highlight or circle each strategy that assisted you to listen and take notes more effectively.*

4

PREPARE FOR EXAMS

Common Types of Exams

Exams in Social Science courses tend to be a combination of objective questions, especially multiple choice items, and essay questions. Rote memorization rarely is adequate to pass exams. Instead, expect that test questions will require higher-level thinking, including application of main ideas and analysis of case studies.

Multiple Choice Questions

Beginning college students frequently are surprised by the difficulty of multiple choice exam questions. Students assume that they will recognize the answer and are confused when the language used in the exam is very different from that in the textbook or lecture notes. At the college level, it is important that you *understand* information and not just memorize what is in your notes or the textbook. Many multiple choice questions on Social Science exams are application questions—that is, you need to utilize information learned in class in a new situation.

Here are some general strategies for tackling multiple choice items:

- *Read carefully*. Look for key words used in the main statement and in the choices of answers.
- *Eliminate*. Narrow down possibilities; cross off answers that you know are wrong.
- *Look for specifics*. Often the more detailed option is the best choice.

- *Look for true options.* Read the main statement with each option, especially when faced with multiple options, such as "a + b" or "none of the above." Then, consider whether that answer is "true" or "false." You are seeking a "true" option(s) as the best answer.
- *Be aware of negatives.* Be careful if a statement contains *not* or *except.*
- *Use clues.* Other questions, especially questions that contain repeated terms or statements, often contain clues about how to answer an item.
- *Guess.* If you are unsure of an answer, take an educated guess in case you run out of time and cannot come back to complete items.

Essay Questions

Exams in the Social Science disciplines often include essay questions. Here are several strategies for answering essay questions:

- *Carefully read the question.* Identify the directive words—those words that indicate the direction or path of your answer. The following chart lists common directive words. The second column explains what type of information you should include in your answer. Directive words provide guidance regarding content and organization of your answer. Note that essay questions often have more than one directive word, such as the example on page 43.
  - ◆ **Directive words:** Use this chart to guide your preparation for essay questions.

Directive Words	What I Should Include in My Answer
Compare	Indicate similarities of ideas; how things are alike (can also include differences).
Contrast	Indicate differences or disparities between or among ideas.
Define	Give a formal definition or meaning, plus further explanation and/or examples.
Critique	Critically analyze and assess an issue; make reference to expert authority or reasons that can support and strengthen your answer.
Describe	Report about, focusing on fundamental characteristics and details (use adjectives/adverbs).

Directive Words	What I Should Include in My Answer
Discuss	Provide points of view or arguments concerning an issue.
Explain	Clarify—provide details; give reasons for—describe why.
Evaluate	Assess or appraise an issue; refer to expert authority or reasons that can support and strengthen your answer.
Identify	Name or label items, often within classifications or categories.
Illustrate	Provide complete examples; add explanations and descriptions.
Justify	Make a case for a statement or point of view by providing reasons and evidence.
List	Place items one after another; note any particular order, such as chronological or level of importance.
Relate	Show how two or more ideas are connected, such as similarities or cause/effect.
Summarize	Go over the main points; review key ideas, omit less important details and examples.
Trace	Order information sequentially; show progression of steps/events.

Source: Lipsky, Sally A. (2008) *College Study: The Essential Ingredients*, 2nd Edition, p. 134. Published by Pearson Prentice Hall, Upper Saddle River, NJ. Reprinted by permission of the publisher.

- *Answer each part of a question in order*. Many questions have multiple parts. Answer each part thoroughly in the order presented. Your instructor will be looking for the same order when reading your answer.
- *Make an outline*. Your answer should include:
  - **Introduction**. Present your thesis. For a short essay, your introduction can be a simple rephrasing of the question.
  - **Body**. Develop each main idea. Include explanations, evidence, examples, and other specifics.
  - **Conclusion**. Summarize your main points.

- *Keep your instructor in mind as you compose your answer.* Remember, your instructor may be assessing hundreds of answers to the same questions. Therefore, your job is to show *clearly* how well you understand the material. Be thorough, yet concise.

- *Use signal or transition words and phrases* to help organize your writing and help your instructor to understand your answer. The chart below provides examples of signal words for each directive word.

Directive Words	Examples of Signal Words and Phrases
Compare	*same as, similarly, likewise, both, as, equal to*
Contrast	*versus, but, on the other hand, nevertheless, in contrast to, instead of*
Define	*to name, labeled by, characterized by*
Critique	*evaluate, critical assessment of, according to*
Describe	*to characterize, labeled with, differentiate, detailed*
Discuss	*a viewpoint, another side of the issue, conversely*
Explain	*to clarify, to detail, shed light on*
Evaluate	*to assess, in appraisal of, in agreement with*
Identify	*a type of, to recognize, distinguished by*
Illustrate	*for instance, such as, to illustrate, a type of, for example*
Justify	*for this reason, because, to verify, to validate*
List	*in addition, also, further, secondarily, next, final, above all, ultimately*
Relate	*linked by, associate with, connected to, as a result, similar to*
Summarize	*in conclusion, to reiterate, in brief, again, to sum up*
Trace	*first, afterward, then, next, followed by, subsequently, currently*

- *Reread your answer, mouthing the words* so that you "hear" your answer. As you reread, ask yourself: Is my answer well-organized and straightforward? Are my main ideas clearly worded at the beginning of each paragraph, followed by adequate supporting details and examples? Are there any grammatical or spelling errors?

Example of Essay Question and Answer

Sociology Exam Question:

One of the greatest social changes during the last half of the 20th century was the rapid influx of women into the labor force. Describe and illustrate how each of the items listed below was affected by this influx of working women. Also, explain the evolution of each item into the 21st century.

1. Married life
2. Child rearing
3. Family income
4. Workplace culture
5. National economic growth

Here's how a student tackled this question:

- Carefully read the question, noting the three directive words: *describe, illustrate,* and *explain.*
- Realized that in order to answer each part of the question, she will *describe* (provide explanations/details) and *illustrate* (provide examples) <u>each</u> of the five listed items. Then, she will *explain* (give reasons for) interrelated development of the five items through the years.
- Constructed a brief outline, which helped to organize her thoughts in preparation for writing her answer, consisting of eight paragraphs:
  <u>Paragraph #1.</u> Short introductory paragraph.

(Continued)

<u>Paragraphs #2–6.</u> Each of these five paragraphs included descriptions and illustrations of how an element was influenced by the influx of working women.

<u>Paragraph #7.</u> A longer paragraph included explanations of the interconnected progression of the five elements through the start of 21st century.

<u>Paragraph #8.</u> Concluding paragraph summed up key points.

- Composed the essay, keeping in mind the need to be thorough yet concise.
- Used signal words: *first, then, characterized by, for example, typically, for instance,* and *in conclusion.*
- When finished writing, she silently reread her essay, checking to make sure that she responded to each part of the question and that her ideas made sense. She corrected several spelling and punctuation errors.

Select, Sort, Solidify

Effective test-taking begins with effective planning. First, find out as much as possible about the test—types of questions, point values, material covered, and suggested study approaches. In addition, see if your instructor will provide sample questions. If need be, seek out a student who had the instructor previously and ask about types of test questions, difficulty level, and recommendations for study.

Strategies to SELECT Content for Exams

Begin by answering the question: *What course information do I need to know for this exam?*

- **Begin studying 5–7 days before an exam.** For a major test, you are more likely to avoid cramming and rote memorization if you start the study process a week early.
- **Review materials daily.** Plan study time so that you are reviewing test-related materials daily—in-class notes, textbook and other readings, and outside assignments.
- **Divide up the material.** Progress at a steady pace throughout the week.

Student Comments

- I recommend using short study periods. I always have had problems concentrating and found that it is much better for me to start studying a week before an exam. By reading and studying a little bit each day, I am able to learn the material much better.

  –Kim

- I have a <u>lot of</u> information to learn in my Art History course. I came close to failing the first test. For the next test, I divided up the information and reviewed it in short study periods. This strategy helped me digest the new material, which made a <u>big</u> impact on my test grade.

  –Gavin

Strategies to SORT Content for Exams

Utilize strategies that help you clarify and understand course content. Answer the question, *How can I summarize, organize, or personalize information that I need to know for the exam?*

- **Combine lecture and text information.** Consolidate key ideas, noting overlapping information. Focus on information that you likely will need to know for the test.
- **Create a visual summary of important ideas.** Use idea maps, charts, timelines, graphs, or Venn diagrams to help you organize main ideas and related details.
- **Create application scenarios.** Make information meaningful and relevant to you.

Strategies to SOLIDIFY Content for Exams

Employ strategies that maximize your ability to remember material for the exam. Answer the question: *What can I do to retain information to use on the exam?*

- **Review briefly.** Skim the information studied in previous sessions before moving on to a new section or topic.
- **Recite aloud.** Repeatedly saying key points out loud helps to store the information in your mind—information that you ultimately want to remember for the exam.

Student Comments

- For Economics, I usually have information scattered through-out my notes. After class I have to look at the text chapter and reorganize my notes. When taking the exam I picture my reorganized notes and can usually recall what I need to know.

  –Cheri

- There is a lot of information in my History course that is not necessary when learning concepts that inevitably will be on the exam. I pick and choose only information that I feel is important, which makes my studying much more efficient.

  –Noah

- **Test your knowledge with practice questions.** Use questions in the chapter or in supplemental materials—jot down your answers. Or, create your own questions that are typical of the type that will be on the exam.
- **Study with others.** Share and discuss key ideas, examples, areas of uncertainty, and study aids. Quiz one another; use practice questions from the text or create your own questions.

Study Groups are small groups of students who meet to review information from a shared class. A well-functioning group can help you learn the material for these reasons:

- You understand the material better if you explain it to some-one else.
- You hear explanations different from your instructor's presentation of content.
- You have specific questions discussed and answered by other people.

Form a study group that is *productive* for you. Avoid a group that socializes too much or that relies heavily on one or two individuals to do the bulk of the work. In order to form a study group that is effective, utilize these criteria:

- ***Ask only serious students***—not just your friends. A group of three or four people usually works the best.
- ***Agree on an organizational plan*** at the beginning, including specific meeting days, beginning and ending times, and locations.
- ***Designate specific assignments*** for each member to prepare for the next meeting.
- ***Designate a person to keep the group on track*** at each meeting; that is, someone to bring the group's attention back to studying whenever members' attention strays.

- Get adequate sleep. Sleep greatly affects your concentration and your memory. Students need an average of 7–9 hours of sleep per night. Be mindful of getting enough sleep each night, especially the week before a major test.

Student Comments

- I like to study with my friends who are in the same class, but <u>only</u> if everyone wants to study. Generally, I am the person who takes charge of the group and keeps everyone on track.

–Ellie

Examples of Review Sheets

Review Chart for Psychology Exam

A student used these steps in preparing for his Psychology exam:

Select

- On Sunday evening, developed a plan to prepare for the upcoming test on Friday.
- Divided the material according to "research methods." Wrote down this plan.

(Continued)

Sort

- Combined information from the text chapter and corresponding lecture notes.
- Created a visual summary chart (below).

Solidify

- Tested his knowledge by answering these questions:
  - For each research method describe a *specific situation* using
    that method (application).
  - Explain *why* each item in the last column is classified as a
    "Disadvantage."
- Went to the weekly peer-led study group on Wednesday
  evening, where he could review with others.
- Was in bed by midnight each night.
- Before class on Friday morning, reviewed the summary chart
  briefly, saying the information out loud to himself.

When to Review	Method	Description	Advantage	Disadvantage
		Research Methods		
Sun.	Observation	systematic study of behavior in natural setting	normal setting	no cause/effect; $$; difficult
Mon.	Case Study	detailed information gathered about specific individuals	detailed information	takes a lot of time
Tues.	Surveys	lots of people answer questions re. behaviors or attitudes	very efficient	random sample; false consensus effect

Tues.	Correlation	relationship between two variables	development of hypotheses	cannot establish cause/effect
Wed.	Experiment	manipulation of variables	can establish cause/effect	bias and error
Thurs.	Review ALL the material!			

Review Chart for History Exam

A student used these steps in preparing for her History exam:

Select

- Since the unit exam was next Friday, she started reviewing lecture notes and corresponding text chapters during the weekend.
- Divided her study time according to the four countries involved.

Sort

- Created a summary chart (next page). Filled in the chart as she reviewed class and text material.

Solidify

- Attended her instructor's review session during Wednesday's class. The instructor gave practice essay questions, which she added to her chart.
- Wrote answers to the essay questions. Shared and discussed answers during Thursday's Supplemental Instruction review session.
- Quickly reviewed the chart again before class on Friday.

Great Depression & Rise of Totalitarianism after World War I

Country	Time Period	Important People	Important Terms & Events	Significance	Essay Practice Questions
Russia	1917–1941	• Czar Nicholas • V.I. Lenin • Stalin • Trotsky	• Russian Revolution • Socialist Party • Bolshevik Revolution • Totalitarianism • Communism	• Czar Nicholas executed. • Lenin and Totalitarian/ Communist party came to power. • Lenin removes Russia from WWI.	• *Trace* development of governments in Russia.
Italy	1920s	• Mussolini	• Black Shirts • March on Rome • The Corporate State • Populist tactics • Fascism	• First dictators in Europe; caused by economic problems.	• *Describe* conditions leading to rise of Mussolini.
Germany	1920–1933	• Hitler • Hindenburg	• War reparations SA • Dawes Plan SS • Nazi party Reichstag • Mein Kampf • Enabling Act • Brown Shirts	• Post-WWI economic crisis & unhappiness allowed Hitler to come to power. • 1933: Hitler elected Chancellor of Germany.	• *Identify* steps Hitler took to power. • *Connect* steps to political and economic conditions.

United States	1924–1933	• Hoover • Franklin Roosevelt • Keynes	• Dawes Plan • Stock Market Crash • Great Depression • Unemployment • Declining Capital • Isolationism • New Deal WPA • Public works projects • Fireside chats	• 1929: Stock market crashes, Wall Street crumbles, Great Depression. • Worldwide financial collapse. • Conditions of depression bring reform in U.S.	• *List* causes of Stock Market Crash. • *List* effects of Great Depression.

Summary Chart

This chart is an overview of test preparation strategies presented in this chapter. Use the chart as you prepare for exams in your Social Science courses.

SELECT	SORT	SOLIDIFY
✓ Begin studying 5–7 days before an exam. ✓ Review materials daily. ✓ Divide up the material.	✓ Combine lecture and text information. ✓ Create a visual summary of important ideas. ✓ Create application scenarios.	✓ Review briefly. ✓ Test your knowledge with practice questions. ✓ Study with others. ✓ Get adequate sleep.

Student Comments

- For my Labor Economics class, I needed to know five ways unions better the economy. I read the material out loud to myself over and over again until I was able to hear myself say this information inside my head. When taking the test, I was able to hear the five ways in my head, just like I had rehearsed.

  –Jess

- When I was a freshman I never studied in advance of an exam, I would stay up late the night before and cram. This didn't work at all! Now I start to study about a week in advance and make sure that I get a good night's sleep before the exam. As a result, my grades are much higher, and I'm not as stressed.

  –JJ

Test Preparation Strategies: Taking Action

Reflect on and apply information presented in this chapter. Follow these five steps, using the sheets on the following page:

1. Fill in the name of your Social Science course and date of the exam.
2. Place a check next to the strategies you will use for this exam.
   - In the **SELECT** column, choose *at least two* of the three strategies.
   - In the **SORT** column, choose *at least two* of the three strategies.
   - In the **SOLIDIFY** column, choose *at least two* of the four strategies.
3. Cut out the sheet. Place it in your notebook or planner, or post it on your computer as a reminder of your plan.
4. Afterward, take a moment to evaluate your success.
5. Repeat these steps for the next test, building on previous approaches that have worked for you.

Course: Exam Date:

SELECT	SORT	SOLIDIFY
___Begin studying 5–7 days before an exam. ___Review materials daily. ___Divide up the material.	___Combine lecture and text information. ___Create a visual summary of important ideas. ___Create application scenarios.	___Review briefly. ___Test your knowledge with practice questions. ___Study with others. ___Get adequate sleep.

Evaluate Your Success: *Highlight or circle each strategy that assisted you with understanding and remembering content for your exam.*

Course: _____ Exam Date: _____

SELECT	SORT	SOLIDIFY
___Begin studying 5–7 days before an exam. ___Review materials daily. ___Divide up the material.	___Combine lecture and text information. ___Create a visual summary of important ideas. ___Create application scenarios.	___Review briefly. ___Test your knowledge with practice questions. ___Study with others. ___Get adequate sleep.

Evaluate Your Success: *Highlight or circle each strategy that assisted you with understanding and remembering content for your exam.*

Course: _____ Exam Date: _____

SELECT	SORT	SOLIDIFY
___Begin studying 5–7 days before an exam. ___Review materials daily. ___Divide up the material.	___Combine lecture and text information. ___Create a visual summary of important ideas. ___Create application scenarios.	___Review briefly. ___Test your knowledge with practice questions. ___Study with others. ___Get adequate sleep.

Evaluate Your Success: *Highlight or circle each strategy that assisted you with understanding and remembering content for your exam.*

5

MAKE IMPROVEMENTS

Checklist of Strategies

An important part of learning college-level course content is to analyze periodically what you have and have not accomplished. For each strategy listed in the chart, honestly assess yourself at this point in the semester.

For Your Social Science Course Are You:	Yes, Often	Some-times	No, Never
Checking the course syllabus regularly?			
Writing down due dates and assignments?			
Skimming notes, homework, and text readings before class?			
Going to each class?			
Listening selectively and writing down key ideas?			
Asking and answering questions during class?			
Reviewing notes soon after each class?			
Making additions and changes as needed to clarify class notes?			

For Your Social Science Course Are You:	Yes, Often	Some- times	No, Never
Keeping up with reading and reviewing assignments weekly?			
Reducing distractions when you read and study?			
Breaking up your reading into sections?			
Focusing on key ideas and connections among these ideas when reading?			
Turning section headings into questions; reading to discover answers?			
Marking and highlighting important text information?			
Creating study guides that summarize and organize text material?			
Using supplemental materials, such as CDs and Websites?			
Seeking out answers to questions, including visiting your instructor during office hours, a graduate assistant, or tutor?			
Using campus resources, such as academic support or tutorial center, writing center, or advising office?			
Beginning to prepare 5–7 days before an exam?			
Combining and summarizing text and lecture material?			
Practicing how to apply the information and answer test questions?			
Reciting aloud as you study?			
Studying with other students who are doing well in the course?			
Sleeping regularly, usually 7–9 hours per night?			

Prioritize and Apply

What do you need to do to improve how effectively and efficiently you are learning information for your Social Science course? From the previous chart, select and prioritize five strategies to apply for your Social Science course. For each item, write a detailed description of how you will implement that strategy *now*.

Strategy	Description of How You Will Apply
1.	
2.	
3.	
4.	
5.	

Review this list weekly throughout the remainder of the semester. Use this as a guide to improve how you read, study, and learn content for your Social Science course.